C0-BLI-299

Masterbuilt Smoker Cookbook

Masterbuilt

Electric Smoker Cookbook

Simple and Delicious

Electric Smoker Recipes for

Your Whole Family

James Houck

Copyright © 2018 James Houck
All rights reserved.

TABLE OF CONTENTS

COPYRIGHT 2018 - ALL RIGHTS RESERVED

This document is geared towards providing exact and reliable information in regards to the topic and issue covered. The publication is sold on the idea that the publisher is not required to render an accounting, officially permitted, or otherwise, qualified services. If advice is necessary, legal or professional, a practiced individual in the profession should be ordered.

From a Declaration of Principles which was accepted and approved equally by a Committee of the American Bar Association and a Committee of Publishers and Associations.

In no way is it legal to reproduce, duplicate, or transmit any part of this document by either electronic means or in printed format. Recording of this publication is strictly prohibited and any storage of this document is not allowed unless with written permission from the publisher. All rights reserved.

The information provided herein is stated to be truthful and consistent, in that any liability, in terms of inattention or otherwise, by any usage or abuse of any policies, processes, or directions contained within is the solitary and utter responsibility of the recipient reader. Under no circumstances will any legal responsibility or blame be held against the publisher for any reparation, damages, or monetary loss due to the information herein, either directly or indirectly.

Respective authors own all copyrights not held by the publisher.

The information herein is offered for informational purposes solely and is universal as so. The presentation of the information is without a contract or any type of guarantee assurance.

The trademarks that are used are without any consent, and the publication of the trademark is without permission or backing by the trademark owner. All trademarks and brands within this book are for clarifying purposes only and are the owned by the owners themselves, not affiliated with this document.

HISTORY OF MASTERBUILT ELECTRIC SMOKER

Show me a man who is diligent in what he does, he will not sit before mere men, such will sit in palaces before the high and mighty of the time. That is the perfect word to describe master built electric smokers. The idea behind the concept of this device was bold and clear from the very inception.

The history behind this concept began with a leap of faith by Dawson McLemore. Everybody has one hobby or passion, such as the case with Mr. Dawson, who turned his passion for welding into a full-fledged family business right from the humble backyard of his building.

He was then into paid employment with Goodyear Tire and Rubber Company. He has a steady income, then, but the desire to support his family pushed him into exploring other possibilities of making ends meet to sustain his family.

One thing stands Dawson out from his contemporaries, he is a man of faith. He operates a life that is totally dependent on the control of the Holy Spirit. While he was driving in one of those days' years past, he was praying for protection and prosperity for his company which is still in the embryo as at them.

Part of the major content of his prayers is for guidance over his business endeavors. As at that time, the business has no clear-cut name. It was during the course of one of this prayer sections (according to direct account) that the name: "Masterbuilt Electric Smoker" became reality.

The name tells a lot about the company. According to him, it implies that the company was built not through the inspiration of a man, but through divine guidance from the highest God himself. That was the real genesis of this company which began from the humble background of a backyard and today has attained an international dimension.

This was purely a family business; today the name rings a bell in industrial circles the world over. The project is built on faith in the in prayers that meets with works. That was the founding principle and even as of today, the culture is still being maintained and sustained.

The workforce is like a family. Great value is put on their well-being; theirs is one of the most motivated workforces that you can ever get into the industry. The commitment to excellence among the staff members is one of the best you can ever find in today's business environment.

A conducive template for a reward of excellence is put in place and that informs the drive among the workforce for excellence at its best. The team of trained experts is excellent on the job; they have been placed higher than the job they do.

Some of the key points which make Masterbuilt electrical smoker the best choice are:

THE COST EFFICIENCY

Despite the design of Masterbuilt electrical smoker being handy and appealing, it is also a great pick with regards to affordability. Buying it does not deprive you of other necessities of daily living. This effective smoker comes between a handy price of $100-$400 and it is the first choice of topmost chefs.

DURABILITY IS ENOUGH TO STAY LONG

Once it is there in your kitchen, it is your responsibility to handle the Masterbuilt electrical smoker with proper care. The durability of any products lies in the hand of the owner, so with this device. If you take proper care, clean and maintain this smoker properly, it is going to live long in with you. Also, it is a perfect product to be used by a family with average members.

ONLY BEST-SMOKED FLAVOR IT IMPARTS

With the Masterbuilt electrical smoker, the users get a plenty of smoking choices. From charcoal smoking to wood smoking, this smoker is apt for all. You can also play with its temperature from low to mild to high when as required. So, use all types of wood ranging from Peachwood to Apple and Oakwood to Pecan. You will have all flavors dancing in your Smoking-Hot pallet.

THREE BEST MASTERBUILT SMOKERS

Now, here I present you the three best Masterbuilt Smokers in the market.

1. MASTERBUILT'S SMOKER WITH FRONT CONTROLLING & VIEWING WINDOW, RF REMOTE CONTROLLING, 40-INCH

If you are looking for a top pick to add in your kitchen, then this 40-inch remote controlled Masterbuilt smoker should be your first choice. It has extra cooking space, external chip feeding chute (fuel and wood, both) and a nicely-sized internal drip tray. This smoker is a total delight for customers who love cooking with great functionality.

Other features of this smoker are; 4-rack system, curvaceous back-ends, and easy-to-use functionality. So, you can say that this smoker is highly convenient and value for your hard-earned money. It will definitely rely on your expectations.

2. THE 30-INCH MASTERBUILT BLACK-COLORED ELECTRIC &ANALOG SMOKER

If you desire style in an electric smoker, then, Masterbuilt offers a 30-inch analog electric smoker is your sure bet. This beautiful smokehouse unit accompanies the look of a smokehouse that incorporates three difference racks for the generation of smoke without compromising with the lack of space.

There is also the luxury of a controllable thermostat that lets you control the temperature at your will without much difficulty. Moreover, the unit offers a pre-installed thermometer that will ensure that your smoking setting is not exceeded. This design also encompasses a tray made of wood chips inside the unit with a supporting water pan. Masterbuilt's electric analog smoking unit is also a representation of the company's intro model. In appearance, it looks like a bare bone, but it is a perfect design that executes the job of a smoking unit.

However, it is prudent to note that an individual will need to unlock the cabinet to add in more smoke chips when needed. This, unfortunately, may lead to the loss of some heat in the smoking process. This is the only perceived shortcoming of this model; aside from that, it is a great buy.

This is a smoking and cooking unit for real with a minimum supporting temperature of 100 degrees F and a maximum 400 degrees F. Do note that you can keep the complete smoking process quite clear and easy if you use aluminum pans that are disposable after smoking the meat. The problem of having to scrub and scrape your cooking utensils is thereby eliminated.

3. MASTERBUILT'S 30-INCH DIGITAL & ELECTRIC SMOKE (BLACK COLORED) WITH TOP CONTROLLER

This model is an upgraded version of the analog model discussed above, that incorporates a few add-ons for an impressive smoking experience. Here too, the smokehouse device accompanies the style used for designing cabinets with the benefits of digital regulators for better precision while reading the temperature and, thankfully, a wood chip feeding system present outside the unit.

Most of the issues that arise with the use of some smokers have to do with temperature control. When this problem surfaces, the food is either overcook to your displeasure or completely burnt to your chagrin. The digital controls included in this model will make sure that a precise temperature (that the desired temperature) is maintained 24/7.

The panel for input settings digitally boasts a commendable timer system featuring a 24-hour clock that offers an autonomous switch off system when your food is cooked. Issues of overcooking are out of the equation. It also has the benefit of wood chips feeding from the outside into the electric smoker. You, therefore, will not undergo the ritual of opening up the main cabinet when you want to refuel. The advantage here is that you will not lose heat when there is a need to refuel the unit. Masterbuilt offers this profound digital and electric smoker accompanied by a top regulator that works well within the temperature scale of 100 to 275 degrees F. You must note at this temperature range that the unit is not meant for fast and hot smoking. Nevertheless, this model is ideal for lower temperatures and is suitable for BBQ, making jerky and cooking some delicious fish.

BENEFITS OF SMOKER

For a consumer to commit in placing an order for a product or service, such must come with some benefits which place it above its other competitors. For this very product which is our object of review, the following are some of the great benefits that are at the beck and call of every customer:

- The first of these rare benefits is that it is so easy to use. There is nothing to be likened to an easy interface between a device and the user.
- From the initial steps of the smoking process to the final clean-up, you cannot find anything more convenient to use as this electric smoking device.
- The issue of a messy charcoal ash to empty or propane tank to change out is completely out of the equation.
- The time as well as the temperature is digitally controlled, and this helps to adequately insulate the unit.
- The accidents are prevented; this takes away the stress of babysitting the cooking.
- The source of energy used is electric energy. This form of energy is cheap and it is not expensive.
- The smoking unit has a whole lot of capacity; you can smoke for the entire family just in one single cooking.

The customer service team of Masterbuilt is extremely sensitive to genuine demands from their customers; you are not likely to encounter any issues in calling for a replacement of the heating element.

Simply load your meat and cover it with a sauce, if desired; then you can consider your smoking done. It is as easy and simple as that.

POULTRY RECIPES USING ELECTRIC SMOKER

STUFFED CHICKEN BREAST IN MASTERBUILT SMOKER

SERVING SIZE: 1
SERVINGS PER RECIPE: 4
CALORIES: 184.8 PER SERVING
COOKING TIME: 2 HOURS

INGREDIENTS:

Chopped crawfish- 1 cup, pre-cooked

Bell pepper- 1/3 cup, red, chopped

Green onion- 1/4 cup, chopped

Parsley- 1/3 cup, chopped

Cheese blend- 1 cup, shredded, Mexican

Mayonnaise- ½ cup

Cajun Hot Sauce- 1-2 teaspoons

Cajun seasoning (Slap Ya' Mama)- 1-2 teaspoons

Chicken breasts- 4, boneless

Moppin' Sauce (Florida Everglades)- ½ cup

NUTRITION INFORMATION:

Carbohydrate – 20.5 g

Protein- 19.9 g

Fat – 2.0 g

Sodium – 475.1 mg

Cholesterol – 42.3 mg

DIRECTIONS:

1. To prepare the Crawfish-stuffed chicken, please ensure that you bring fresh chicken breast just before cooking. It will keep the prepared dish fresh for long.

2. Now, let us prepare the brine. To prepare it, take a large and deep pot. Into the pot, add ½ gallon water, kosher salt (1/2 cup), and brown sugar (1/3 cup). Add the chicken breast and leave the whole in the refrigerator for a night.

3. Take out the chicken breasts soaked overnight in brine. Take a paper towel and pat it dry.

4. Leave the chicken aside and prepare the stuffing. To prepare the stuffing, take the boiled Crawfish, Green Onion, Red Pepper, Cheese and Parsley in a bowl. Add in the hot sauce and Mayonnaise. Give it a good hand-mix and keep it aside.

5. To prepare the stuffed chicken, you would need to soften the breasts. To do this, wrap the breasts in a plastic film and use a mallet.

6. Beat the chicken breasts slowly, so that all the vacuum is removed from the chicken breasts. Remember, you must gently soften it, not tear it.

7. Now, remove the film from the soften chicken breasts and sprinkle Cajun Seasoning over it. With your hands, nicely rub the seasoning over chicken breasts so that it is nicely seasoned.

8. Now, take the stuffing (approximately 4-5 tablespoons), or depending upon the size of the chicken breast and keep it on the top.

9. Roll up the chicken breasts and nicely seal it so that the mixture does not pour out.

10. Meanwhile, prepare the Masterbuilt smoker and add Sassafras woodchips. The temperature of the smoker should be 275 degrees Fahrenheit.

11. Into the heated smoker, place the rolled-up Cajun seasoned chicken breasts.

12. Insert a thermometer probe to check the internal temperature.

13. When the temperature reaches, 160 degrees Fahrenheit, wipe it off with the Moppin' Sauce. The chicken will take about an hour and half to reach the desired temperature of 160 degrees.

14. Now, cook it for 30 minutes more until the temperature reaches, 165 degrees F.

15. After 30 minutes, remove Chicken Breasts from Masterbuilt Smoker and keep it aside for about 10-15 minutes.

16. Serve it and enjoy!

BEER SMOKED CHICKEN IN MASTERBUILT SMOKER

SERVING SIZE: ½ POUND PER PERSON
SERVINGS PER RECIPE: 6
CALORIES: 127.6 PER SERVING
COOKING TIME: 3 HOURS

INGREDIENTS:

Whole chicken- 1, (3 1/2 pound)

Dry rub (any of your choice)- 1/4 cup

Beer can- 1, (gluten-free beer)

Marinade- 3 cups

NUTRITION INFORMATION:

Carbohydrate – 0.3 g

Protein- 21.6 g

Fat – 0.8 g

Sodium – 66.8 mg

Cholesterol – 66.9 mg

DIRECTIONS:

1. Start by rinsing the chicken cavity and removing giblets.
2. Take the dry rub or seasoning of your choice and properly rub inside and out of the chicken.
3. While rubbing, press the seasoning onto the surface of the chicken and allow it to rest in the refrigerator for an hour.
4. Meanwhile, prepare the Masterbuilt Smoker and empty the beer can in the drip pan.
5. In the can, fill up the marinade and put that can into the cavity of the chicken.
6. Now, keep aside the chicken and prepare the Masterbuilt Electric Smoker. You have to keep it on indirect heat mode and use the woodchips of your liking.
7. For this particular recipe, I would recommend, Applewood; however, if that is unavailable, you can choose one from, Hickory, Mesquite, or Oakwood.
8. Going further, maintain the temperature of the smoker something between 225 degrees F and 275 degrees F.
9. It is time now to place the chicken on Smoker Grill with Beer Can as the base. Cook the chicken for at least 3 hours.
10. If you have used a dripping pan filled with beer and water, that is great; but if you have not done so, then try basting the chicken with the marinade you have.
11. Also, to see the internal temperature of the chicken, poke a thermometer in the thickest part of the meat and wait for the thermometer to read 165 degrees F.
12. If the thermometer reads 165 degrees F, your chicken in beer is ready.
13. Now, once done, remove the chicken from the smoker and let it rest for additional 20 minutes.
14. After 20 minutes, take out your knife and fork and just binge on.

SMOKED CHICKEN WITH APPLE-GINGER MARINADE

SERVING SIZE: ½ POUND PER PERSON
SERVINGS PER RECIPE: 6
CALORIES: 127.6 PER SERVING
COOKING TIME: 2 HOURS

INGREDIENTS:

Rice Vinegar - 1/2 cup, NAKANO Seasoned

Apple juice (concentrate)- 1/2 cup, frozen

Tamari sauce- 3 tablespoons, gluten-free

Natural ketchup- 3 tablespoons

Fresh ginger- 1 piece (2 inches), grated

Dijon mustard- 2 tablespoons

Olive oil- 2 tablespoons

Black pepper- 1/4 teaspoon, ground

Lemon- 1, zest and juice

Chicken- 1 (3 pound)

Beer can- 1

NUTRITION INFORMATION:

Carbohydrate – 0.3 g

Protein- 21.6 g

Fat – 0.8 g

Sodium – 66.8 mg

Cholesterol – 66.9 mg

DIRECTIONS:

1. Take a small mixing bowl and mix all ingredients, including rice vinegar, apple juice, tamari sauce, natural ketchup, ginger, Dijon Mustard, Olive oil, black pepper, and lemon.

2. The prepared mixture is marinade which you will use to marinade the chicken.

3. So, take the chicken and empty its cavity. Rinse it with running water and nicely dry it using the paper towel. Once dried, use the marinade to cover the chicken. Put that marinated chicken in the refrigerator and forget for 2 hours. For better flavor, you can even leave it for 24 hours.

4. Now, on the next day, take out the chicken from the refrigerator and keep the rest of the marinade aside. You can later use it while smoking the chicken for basting.

5. So, as your chicken is marinated, you will now require the smoker to smoke it finally. Therefore, start with heating the smoker and placing the woodchips for flavor. I would recommend Applewood.

6. The temperature of the Masterbuilt Smoker should be 250 degrees F and the mode should be direct. Now, place the chicken on the rack and use a drip pan filled with beer and water.

7. While the chicken is being smoked, keep an eye on the doneness of the chicken. You will require 185 degrees F as an internal temperature for the doneness of the chicken.

8. To check, you will need to insert a thermometer probe in the thickest part of the chicken.

9. Once the internal temperature is 185 degrees F, the chicken is ready.

10. You can enjoy it with your family and friends.

SMOKED TURKEY WITH FLAVORS OF MIXED HERBS

SERVING SIZE:
SERVINGS PER RECIPE:
CALORIES: 276.4 PER SERVING
COOKING TIME: MINUTES

INGREDIENTS:

Turkey- 14 pound

Dried thyme- 2 teaspoons

Powdered sage- 1 teaspoon

Dried oregano- 2 tablespoons

Paprika- 2 tablespoons

Sea salt- 2 tablespoons

Black pepper- 1-1/2 tablespoons cracked

Dried rosemary- 1 tsp.

Onion- 1 teaspoon

Garlic powder- 1 teaspoon

Orange zest- ½ of the orange

Olive Oil (EVOO)- 1/4 Cup

Apple Cider- 1/2 Cup

Water- 1/2 Cup

Applewood Chips

NUTRITION INFORMATION:

Carbohydrate – 0.1 g

Protein- 30.7 g

Fat – 16.2 g

Sodium – 78.2 mg

Cholesterol – 88.1 mg

DIRECTIONS:

1. To prepare the smoked turkey, you will require a perfect size of Turkey that could fit in your electric smoker. Once you buy the turkey, you will require to thaw it nice and slow.

2. Although, if you choose a refrigerated turkey, you will still have to leave it for 3 days to completely thaw.

3. Once the process is complete, clean the turkey and remove giblets and neck. After cleaning it, rinse it with water and let it dry.

4. Meanwhile, it is kept to dry, prepare the brine mixing ½ cup or sugar and salt to water. It should be measured every gallon until the turkey is fully submerged. Allow the turkey to rest for 14 hours.

5. After 14 hours, take the turkey out of the brine and rinse it. The rinsing should be done with cold water. As you have rinsed the turkey, dry it with the help of a paper towel and keep it aside.

6. Meanwhile, prepare the Masterbuilt Smoker for direct heating at a temperature 225 degrees F.

7. As the smoker is heating, prepare the herb mixture by mixing all the herbs in a mixing bowl. With this prepared mix, rub the turkey all over the outside surface. For better flavor, force the dry rub on the skin of Turkey.

8. Also, for the second layering of rub, add the EVOO and zest of an orange in the herb mix. Again, nicely apply the seasoning all over the outside surface and let the turkey rest.

9. Meanwhile, you take a water pan and add cider vinegar with an equal quantity of water. Place the water pan in the bottom of Masterbuilt Smoker. The pan must be half filled.

10. Also, place a drip just a shelf below Turkey so that it could collect all the juices and drippings during the smoking process. Last but not the least, add the Applewood chips in the box and the smoker is ready to place the turkey.

11. Now, while it is the time to place the turkey in the smoker, you will have to tightly tuck the wings beneath the turkey. After tucking the wings, place it on the rack and seal the door.

12. The timer of the smoker should be set at 6.5 hours. To check the doneness of the turkey, insert a thermometer probe in the thickest part and wait for it to display 165 degrees F.

13. While the smoking process is on, check the turkey every hour for a smoke; if you see less smoke, add more Applewood chips.

14. After 6.5 hours, when the meat thermometer reads 165 degrees F, remove the smoked turkey and let it rest on cutting board for 20 minutes.

15. After 20 minutes, carve beautifully and juices pieces of turkey and serve.

16. You can serve herb-smoked sweet potatoes as a side dish to this flavorful turkey.

SMOKED GAME HENS IN MASTERBUILT SMOKER

SERVING SIZE: 1/2 PIECE OF A HEN
SERVINGS PER RECIPE: 8
CALORIES: 160 PER SERVING
COOKING TIME: 2 HOURS 50 MINUTES

INGREDIENTS:

Game hens- 4, whole Cornish

Olive oil (EVOO)- 1/4 cup

Oranges- 3, quarters

Sea salt- 4 tsp.

Black pepper- 2 tsp, cracked

Dried thyme- 2 tsp

Fruitwood chips

Water

Butcher's twine

NUTRITION INFORMATION:

Carbohydrate – 0 g

Protein- 14 g

Fat – 11 g

Sodium - 520 mg

Cholesterol – 50 mg

DIRECTIONS:

1. Clean the hens and rinse them with water. After rinsing them with water, use a paper towel to dry them.
2. After that, allow the hens to stay at room temperature; you can leave them for maximum 30-minutes.
3. While the chicken is resting, prepare the seasoning. Set the Masterbuilt smoker to 250 degrees F. For the smoky flavors, add Fruitwood chips to chip tray and add water to the water bowl. It should be filled up to halfway.
4. Now, as you have already prepared the seasoning, combine it with EVOO and rub in the cavity and on the outside surface of each hen.
5. After rubbing the seasoning, stuff each hen with oranges, 3 quarters and tie the legs with twine.
6. Place the hens on the smoker rack and nicely tuck their wings under their trunk. Smoke them for 2 and a half hours and check for internal temperature. It should be 165 degrees F.
7. If required keep adding the woodchips for continuous smoking.
8. Once done, remove hens and let them rest for 20 minutes.
9. Discard the organs and cut them into halves.
10. Serve them with side dishes of your choice.

SEAFOOD RECIPES USING ELECTRIC SMOKER

SMOKED SALMON WITH VODKA FLAVOR

SERVING SIZE:
SERVINGS PER RECIPE:
CALORIES: 117 PER SERVING
COOKING TIME: 4 HOURS

INGREDIENTS:

Salmon filet- 1 pound, whole (bones and skin removed)

Vodka- 1 shot, unflavored

Kosher salt- 1/4 cup

Turbinado sugar- 1/4 cup, brown

Black pepper (cracked)- 2 tablespoons

Fresh dill- 1 bunch, chopped

Lemon- ½, thinly sliced

Alder woodchips

NUTRITION INFORMATION:

Carbohydrate – 0 g

Protein- 22.5 g

Fat – 12.3 g

Sodium – 666.8 mg

Cholesterol – 19.6 mg

DIRECTIONS:

1. Prepare fish by cutting it in half and stacking on each other. Further, take a glass tray and fill it with Vodka. In the vodka, place Salmon fillets and rub its surface with a mixture of salt, sugar, and pepper.
2. Now, gently press down dill on the surface of the salmon and cover it with plastic wrap. The plastic wrap should tighten so that it tucks the fish down in the tray.
3. Wrap one more layer to seal the fish tightly in the tray and leave the tray in the refrigerator overnight. It could be approximate 12 hours.
4. After 12 hours, remove the tray from the refrigerator and take out the salmon, discarding the liquid. Clean the fillet with cold water and remove all the rubbed seasoning including the lemon, herbs, etc.
5. Now, with the help of a paper towel, nicely clean fillets and keep them aside for 2 hours. It will be completely dry till then.
6. Meanwhile, fillets are resting, soak the Alder woodchips in water.
7. Take out the grill from the Masterbuilt Smoker and rub its olive oil. After oiling the grill, place fillets on it.
8. Now, heat the Masterbuilt Smoker and the temperature should be 160 degrees F.
9. Place the grill into the smoker and set the cook time for 4 hours. Also, in every 45 minutes, keep checking for the smoke. If it is less, add more wood chips.
10. Although the fish will attain a soft texture within a cook time of 2.5 hours, yet some people it with a firmer texture. Therefore, cook it for 1.5 more hours and check for its doneness. If the fish has 135 degrees F internal temperature, it is done.
11. Keep it outside the smoker for 15 minutes and it is ready to eat.

SMOKED FISH CROSTINI

SERVING SIZE: 1
SERVINGS PER RECIPE: 24
CALORIES: 70 PER SERVING
COOKING TIME: 25 MINUTES

INGREDIENTS:

FOR SMOKED SALMON

Water- 1 gallon

Kosher salt- 1 cup

White sugar- 1 cup

Brown sugar- 1 cup

Lemon pepper- as per taste

dry fish seasoning mix- 3 ounce

Black pepper- Freshly ground (to taste)

Garlic cloves- 4, crushed

Pepper sauce- 1 dash

Lemons- 4, crushed and sliced

Oranges- 2 crushed and sliced

Lime- 1, crushed and sliced

Yellow onion- 1 large, sliced

Salmon

FOR CROSTINI

Baguette (from 1 small loaf)- 24 thin slices

Olive oil- 2 tablespoons

Cream cheese- 4 ounces

Fresh dill- 2 tablespoons, chopped

Prepared horseradish- 1 tablespoon

Kosher salt

Black pepper

Smoked salmon- 4 ounces

NUTRITION INFORMATION:

Carbohydrate – 6 g

Protein- 4 g

Fat – 4 g

Sodium - 145 mg

Cholesterol – 12 mg

DIRECTIONS:

FOR SMOKED SALMON

1. Take 1-gallon water in a large size mixing bowl and add Kosher Salt, Brown Sugar, White Sugar, Lemon, Pepper, Parsley, Hot Sauce, Seasoning mix, Garlic, Lemons, Oranges, onion, and Lime.
2. In this brine, add the Salmon and cover it with foil. Leave this overnight.
3. On the next day, take out Salmon from the brine and rinse with cold water. Keep the salmon aside on a paper towel to absorb the moisture. Meanwhile, you prepare the Masterbuilt Smoker by adding Woodchip of your choice.
4. Keep the temperature to 225 degrees F and smoke the fish until the internal temperature is reached to 140 degrees. Once the temperature is reached at 140 degrees F, take out the salmon and place it on the chopping board.
5. Do not cut it immediately, however, leave it for 15 minutes.
6. After 15 minutes, cut it in the way, you wanted it in Crostini.

FOR SALMON CROSTINI

1. To make the Salmon crostini, heat your oven to 400 degrees F and line a baking tray with baguette brushed with olive oil both the sides.
2. Bake these baguettes until they golden brown; it would approximately take 5 minutes of yours.
3. Now, prepare a mix of mixing cream cheese, dill, horseradish, pepper, and Salt.
4. Assemble Salmon Crostini by placing an equal amount of prepared cream cheese mixture on each slice of Baguette topped with Salmon.
5. For garnishing, sprinkle dill on the top.
6. Your delicious Salmon crostini is ready to munch on.

SCHMANCY SMOKED SALMON

SERVING SIZE: ½ POUND EACH
SERVINGS PER RECIPE: 4
CALORIES: 111 PER SERVING
COOKING TIME: MINUTES

INGREDIENTS:

Salmon fillets- 2 pounds (Fillets must have same thickness)

Hot water- 1/2 cup

Salt- 1/4 pound

White sugar- 1/4 cup, granulated

Garlic powder- 2 tablespoons

Black pepper- 2 tablespoons, ground

Cold water- 1/2 gallon

Paper bag- 1, clean brown

NUTRITION INFORMATION:

Carbohydrate – 3 g

Protein- 8 g

Fat – 8 g

Sodium - 479 mg

Cholesterol – 0 mg

DIRECTIONS:

1. The process of making smoked salmon start by checking whether there are any bones left or not. To check, just run your fingers over the flesh.
2. If there is no pin bone, it is good to go; otherwise, drape the salmon over the bowl's edge and with the help of tweezers, remove pin bones.
3. Once done, choose a container for bringing the fish. The container needs to large enough to nicely hold the brine as well as the meat. Also, the container should not be of metals like Aluminum, Cast Iron and Copper. These metals will too easily react with salt. Therefore, you are not able to find a suitable container, Zipper bags will work wonders.
4. Now, to prepare the brine, mix hot water, salt, black pepper, and garlic with other ingredients and give all a good mix.
5. In this brine, add Salmon fillets and making sure that the fillets are fully submerged in brine. You have to keep the container in the refrigerator for at least 24 hours. Also, before putting the container in the refrigerator, make sure you have properly covered it with a plastic wrap.
6. Now, after 24 hours, take out fillets of the fish from the brine and place them on the brown paper; they should be kept skin-side down. Keeping them this way will help you remove away the skin easily.
7. Now, glaze fish fillets with sugar and keep them in the smoker for 60 minutes. The temperature of Masterbuilt Smoker should be 225 degrees F.
8. As the fillets will reach the stage of doneness, the liquid will ooze out of the surface.
9. For betterment, just keep a meat thermometer handy; check the fillets for an internal temperature of 140 degrees F and if the temperature is reached, remove them from the smoker
10. After removing the fillets, let them rest for 15 minutes. Once they are cooled, peel out the paper from the skin-side and look for the dark flesh. Scrap it out and enjoy the smoked salmon.

SMOKED SHRIMP IN MASTERBUILT SMOKER

SERVING SIZE: 3-4
SERVINGS PER RECIPE: 25
CALORIES: 107.3 PER SERVING
COOKING TIME: MINUTES

INGREDIENTS:

Shrimp- 3 pounds, headless or shell on

Butter- 1 1/2 sticks

Worcestershire sauce- 1/3 cup

Hot sauce- 1/4 cup (mild-to-medium)

Crab boil- 1 teaspoon, liquid

Black pepper (cracked)- 1/8 cup

Cayenne pepper- 1/8 cup

Sweet basil- 1 tablespoon

Oregano- 1 tablespoon

Cumin- 1 teaspoon

Paprika- 1 teaspoon

Nutmeg- 1 teaspoon

Baking pan (Smoker-safe and shallow pan to hold all the 25 shrimp)

NUTRITION INFORMATION:

Carbohydrate – 0 g

Protein- 10 g

Fat – 2 g

Sodium - 440 mg

Cholesterol – 120 mg

DIRECTIONS:

1. Start by melting butter in the Smoker-Safe pan. Heat it in the smoker until the butter is soft. When but is soft and melted, remove the pan from smoker and pour in the mentioned quantity of Worcestershire Sauce, Crab oil, and Hot sauce.

2. Now, add all 25 shrimps in the pan and nice mix. The mix of butter, hot sauce, Worcestershire sauce and crab oil should be nicely stuck to the surface of the shrimp.

3. Further, take all the dry ingredients in a bowl and sprinkle over the shrimp. Either use tow wooden spatula or your hands (gloved) to give the whole a good hand-mix. Toss them gently until the shrimp are nicely coated with marinade and rub.

4. Now, preheat your Masterbuilt Electric Smoker to 230 degrees F and add your choice of wood chips. I would recommend Pecan or Apple. You can even use a mix of both.

5. So, as you are done deciding, add the woodchips in the chute and wait until the chips start smoking.

6. Once you see smoke, place the shrimp and smoke until they are opaque and curled up. It would take all around 60 minutes.

7. In between the smoking, you can turn the shrimp, it will help reach flavor everywhere.

8. After 60 minutes, spoon out shrimp from the pan and pour on the platter. Pour some extra sauce over shrimp and serve them with Caesar Salad and French bread with crust.

RICE-PINEAPPLE PILAF AND SMOKED TILAPIA WITH JERK SEASONING

SERVING SIZE: 1
SERVINGS PER RECIPE: 4
CALORIES: 261.1 PER SERVING
COOKING TIME: 2 HOURS 30 MINUTES

INGREDIENTS:

Tilapia- 1 pound, around 4 fillets

Allspice- 1 tsp

Nutmeg- 1 tsp

Cinnamon- 1 tsp

Garlic powder- 1 tsp

Ground ginger- 1 tsp

Black pepper- 1 tsp

Cayenne pepper- 1/2 tsp

Ground cloves- 1/2 tsp

Salt- 2 tsp

Oil- 2 tbsp.

Pineapple- 1, whole

Red pepper- 1, cored and nicely diced

Green onions- 6, sliced

Garlic cloves- 2, minced

Cooked rice- 6 cups

Cilantro- 3 tbsp., minced

NUTRITION INFORMATION:

Carbohydrate – 20.9 g

Protein- 36.5 g

Fat – 3.3 g

Sodium – 741.2 mg

Cholesterol – 82.3 mg

DIRECTIONS:

1. Start by preparing jerk seasoning and mix together all the dry spices, including Allspice, Cinnamon, Nutmeg, Garlic Powder, Black Pepper, Ground Ginger, Cayenne pepper, Salt and Ground Cloves.
2. Now, rub this seasoning all over the surface of the fish.
3. Heat Masterbuilt Electric Smoker to the temperature 275 degrees F and place wood chips in the chute. You can choose any of the chips like Alder, Hickory, Apple, etc.
4. As the smoker is prepared, place the Tilapia Fillets on the smoker rack and put it in the Masterbuilt Smoker. Also, insert a thermometer to check the internal temperature, which should be 145 degrees F. This internal temperature will be reached in 2 hours.
5. After 2 hours, remove the fish from the smoker and keep it aside.
6. Meanwhile, prepare the pineapple and cut it in half longitudinally. Now, scoop out all the flesh of pineapple and chop the flesh into small chunks. You can discard the hardcore.
7. Now, heat a wok on medium heat and add in red pepper, garlic clove, and green onion.
8. Sauté them until they are translucent. Then, add pineapple and sauté for additional 5 minutes.

9. In the wok, add in the already cooked rice and cilantro. Fry it for 10 minutes more and heat the rice properly. To heat it properly, you must keep stirring it often, scraping the skillet's bottom to avoid the rice from sticking.

10. Remove the wok from heat. Crumble the Tilapia fish which you smoked with jerk spices. The chunks should be medium sized to match the rice pilaf.

11. Now, for the final presentation, add the prepared rice in scooped out pineapple. Serve it hot!

PORK RECIPES USING ELECTRIC SMOKER

OAK WOOD SMOKED PORK LOIN

SERVING SIZE: 1 PLATE
SERVINGS PER RECIPE: 8
CALORIES: 276.8 PER SERVING
COOKING TIME: 480 MINUTES

INGREDIENTS:

Oakwood chips- 3 cups

Brown sugar- 2 tbsp.

Coriander- 1 tsp, ground

Orange peel- 1 tsp, finely shredded

Paprika- 1 tsp

Black pepper- ¼ tsp

Ground ginger- ½ tsp

Pork loin- 2-pound, single roast, boneless

NUTRITION INFORMATION:

Carbohydrate – 8.1 g

Protein- 37.5 g

Fat – 9.3 g

Sodium – 774.5 mg

Cholesterol – 105.4 mg

DIRECTIONS:

1. Give a soak to the oak wood for about 1 or 2 hours. During that time, you can prepare the meat by trimming the fat. Then, place the bag of the meat in a dish.
2. Take a small bowl to mix orange peel, brown sugar, paprika, coriander, ginger, pepper, and salt.
3. Use this mixture to rub all over the meat. You can use your fingers to ensure that every area and part of the meat gets covered with the mixture.
4. Now, let the meat rest for about 40 minutes at the room temperature. Or, you can put it in the refrigerator for about 3 to 4 hours.
5. After doing that, prepare your Masterbuilt Smoker with the oak wood pieces.
6. Place the coal near the drip pan of the smoker. Then, make sure that the heat setting is at medium-low. Put half of the total chips on the coal placed earlier.
7. Shift the meat above the pan and let it grill until you obtain an internal temperature of about 155 degrees.
8. Make sure that you include the rest of the wood chips after the halftime of the cooking.
9. Shift the meat from the smoker and let it rest for about 20 minutes.

SMOKED BOSTON PORK BUTT WITH APPLE JUICE

SERVING SIZE: 1 PLATE
SERVINGS PER RECIPE: 20
CALORIES: 745.8 PER SERVING
COOKING TIME: 12 HOURS, 15 MINUTES

INGREDIENTS:

Boston pork butt- 1

Apple juice- 1 spray bottle

Rub- 1 cup, all-purpose

NUTRITION INFORMATION:

Carbohydrate – 8.9 g

Protein- 53.3 g

Fat – 54.4 g

Sodium - 3039 mg

Cholesterol – 213.1 mg

DIRECTIONS:

1. Prepare the pork butt by removing the fat from the top and the bottom part of the butt.
2. Use the rub with your hands to reach all parts of the butt.
3. Prepare your Masterbuilt Smoker for the smoking process. Include fruitwood pieces and let the smoking temperature reach the level of about 225 to 250 degrees.
4. Place the butt in the smoker and let it cook for about 5 to 6 hours.
5. You can also choose to grill with the availability of indirect heating. But make sure you keep on rotating the butt after every 1 hour. This will help in cooking thoroughly in all directions evenly.
6. During the smoking process, use the apple juice spray to cover the butt after every 1 hour during the first 4 hours of cooking. You can also add more rub to complement the apple juice.
7. Now, shift the pork butt to a pan made of aluminium. Wrap this pan with a foil to tightly cover the meat.
8. Place the meat back in the Masterbuilt Smoker and let the meat reach a temperature of about 200 internally. It should take about 11 to 12 hours to obtain this temperature.
9. Now, shift the pan of pork but from the smoker and leave it to rest for about 1 to 1 ½ hour.
10. Pull the meat and serve with burgers.

PORK TENDERLOIN WITH BBQ SAUCE

SERVING SIZE: 1 PLATE
SERVINGS PER RECIPE: 2
CALORIES: 337.7 PER SERVING
COOKING TIME: 3 HOURS, 5 MINUTES

INGREDIENTS:

Pork tenderloin- 1

BBQ sauce- ¼ cup

Rub- 3 tbsp., your favorite

NUTRITION INFORMATION:

Carbohydrate – 2.4 g

Protein- 45.1 g

Fat – 12.5 g

Sodium – 638.9 mg

Cholesterol – 119.4 mg

DIRECTIONS:

1. Choose maple or hickory wood and let it soak for at least 1 hour.
2. Prepare the Masterbuilt Smoker for the cooking process at 225 degrees F.
3. During that time, you can take out the fat from the pork tenderloin. Also, remove the silver skin if you find any.
4. Choose your favorite rub mixture and carefully layer it all over the pork tenderloin. You can use your hands to ensure that the mixture reaches all parts of the tenderloin.
5. After that, you can place the meat in the smoker. Let the meat cook at the low temperature for about 3 to 4 hours. Make sure that the internal temperature of the meat achieves a level of 145 degrees F.
6. When about 2 ½ hours get completed in the smoker, use a brush to cover the BBQ sauce all over the meat. In 30 extra minutes of cooking, the BBQ sauce will blend in the flavor of the meat.
7. After cooking, you can take out the meat from the smoker. Let it rest for about ½ hour before cut and serve the meat.

SPICY SMOKED PORK BUTT

SERVING SIZE: 1 PLATE
SERVINGS PER RECIPE: 10
CALORIES: 219.3 PER SERVING
COOKING TIME: 480 MINUTES

INGREDIENTS:

Pork butt- 8 lbs.

FOR RUB:

Black pepper- ¼ cup

Paprika- ¾ cup

White sugar- ¼ cup

Kosher salt- ¼ cup

Chili powder- 2 tbsp.

Brown sugar- ¼ cup

Onion powder- 2 tbsp.

Garlic powder- 2 tbsp.

Cayenne pepper- 1 tsp

FOR INJECTION:

Apple cider vinegar- ¼ cup

Apple cider- 2 cups

Brown sugar- ¼ cup

White sugar- ¼ cup

Kosher salt- ¼ cup

Garlic powder- 1 tbsp.

Onion powder- 1 tbsp.

Chili pepper- 1 tsp

Ground cumin- 12 tsp

Black pepper- ½ tsp

FOR SPRITZ:

Apple cider vinegar- 1 tbsp.

Apple cider- 1 cup

Prepared rub- 1 tbsp.

NUTRITION INFORMATION:

Carbohydrate – 2.4 g

Protein- 1 g

Fat – 0.1 g

Sodium – 1473.9 mg

Cholesterol – 0 mg

DIRECTIONS:

1. Mix all the ingredient for the injection well and fill up the injection as well as the rub by using the given ingredients.
2. Use the prepared injection to properly fill the pork butt. Cover the pork and let it refrigerate for about 5 hours until it reaches a temperature of 40 degrees. This will make smoking much effective.
3. After that, you can use the prepared rub to completely coat the meat. Use your hands for proper coverage. Let the meat rest with the rub until it gets a little darker on the surface.
4. Choose the wood chips and let them soak for about 30 to 40 minutes in water.
5. Prepare the Masterbuilt Smoker to obtain a heat of about 275 to 325 degrees F.
6. After getting the desired temperature, shift the dried wood chips in the smoker.
7. Put apple cider and water in the water tray. Then, put the pork at the center of the rack.
8. Start smoking and keep on adding more wood pieces after every hour of cooking.
9. When you see that the internal temperature of the pork is about 160 degrees, take it out carefully.
10. Now, you need to melt some butter in an oven. And place the meat with a little rub in an aluminum foil. Also, include a coat of brown sugar. Then, pour the melted butter on the meat too.
11. Follow the same process on the top side of the meat. Then, wrap the meat with the aluminum foil and seal it properly.
12. Smoke the meat for another 40 to 45 minutes to get a temperature of about 190 degrees.
13. Take the meat out from the smoker and let it rest for about 30 minutes. Then, you can start pulling.

HONEY CAJUN SMOKED HAM

SERVING SIZE: 1 PLATE
SERVINGS PER RECIPE: 8
CALORIES: 212.3 PER SERVING
COOKING TIME: 45 MINUTES

INGREDIENTS:

Brown sugar- ¼ cup, dark

Honey- ¼ cup

Precooked ham- 10 lbs.

Dijon mustard- 1 tbsp.

Hickory wood chips

Cajun butter- 8 oz.

Cloves- 2 tbsp., whole

NUTRITION INFORMATION:

Carbohydrate – 27.3 g

Protein- 9.7 g

Fat – 7.2 g

Sodium - 393 mg

Cholesterol – 23 mg

DIRECTIONS:

1. Mix mustard, honey, brown sugar and then rub it all over the ham.
2. Make a scratch of about 5 inches on the back portion of the ham. Insert whole cloves inside that cavity.
3. Now, use an injection to insert Cajun butter. Make sure you insert the butter very deep in the ham.
4. Place the marinated ham in a bowl and prepare the Masterbuilt Smoker.
5. Set the temperature of the smoker at 350 degrees F and let it get ready.
6. Put the meat in the smoker and let it stay there for about 30 minutes without the cover.
7. Then, smoke the meat until you obtain an internal temperature of about 140 to 150-degrees F.
8. After the cooking, you can shift the meat to a pan and pour the rest of the marinade over it. Slice the ham into pieces and serve warm.

INDIAN STYLE PORK ROAST

SERVING SIZE: 1 PLATE
SERVINGS PER RECIPE: 12
CALORIES: 296.9 PER SERVING
COOKING TIME: 360 MINUTES

INGREDIENTS:

Roast pork- 6 lbs.

Cumin- 1 tsp

Cardamom seeds- ½ tsp

Coriander- 1 tsp

Star anise- 4

Black peppercorns- ½ tsp

Red chili- ½ tsp, ground

Turmeric powder- 1 tsp

Canola oil- 4 tbsp.

Salt- according to taste

NUTRITION INFORMATION:

Carbohydrate – 12.3 g

Protein- 32.4 g

Fat – 11.9 g

Sodium – 650.8 mg

Cholesterol – 80.5 mg

DIRECTIONS:

1. Use all the spices to great a mixture. You can use a blender to ensure the consistency of the mixture.
2. Include the oil in the prepared mixture of spices. Coat this mixture using your hands all over the pork roast. Make sure you cover all parts of the roast thoroughly.
3. Place the pork in the refrigerator for about 12 to 24 hours.
4. Prepare your Masterbuilt Smoker by including a mixture of apple and hickory wood chips. Let the smoker reach the temperature of about 225 degrees F.
5. Place the meat inside the smoker and let it smoke until you obtain an internal temperature of about 160 degrees F.
6. Take out the meat and cover it with an aluminium foil. Leave to rest for about 30 minutes and then prepare to serve.

PORK SAUSAGE

SERVING SIZE: 1 PLATE
SERVINGS PER RECIPE: 12
CALORIES: 221.6 PER SERVING
COOKING TIME: 480 MINUTES

INGREDIENTS:

Hamburger meat- 5 lbs.

Tender quick- 5 tsp

Sugar cure- 2 tbsp.

Mustard seeds- 2 tsp

Peppercorns- 2 tsp

Liquid smoke- 2 tsp

Garlic powder- 1 tsp

Red pepper- 2 tsp, crushed

Coarse pepper- 2 tsp

NUTRITION INFORMATION:

Carbohydrate – 18.9 g

Protein- 9.2 g

Fat – 13.4 g

Sodium – 114.3 mg

Cholesterol – 30.1 mg

DIRECTIONS:

1. Take a large pan to mix all the ingredients and let it refrigerate for about 4 days. Make sure you mix it well each day. When you are ready to cook, prepare your Masterbuilt Smoker by adding soaked and dried wood chips. Preheat the smoker to obtain a temperature of about 225 degrees F. During that time, you can work on your meat rolls.

2. Create meat rolls of the mixture and smoke them in the Masterbuilt Smoker at a temperature of about 225 degrees F. This should take about 8 to 10 hours for complete cooking.

3. Keep on checking the meat after every ½ hour during the smoking. You can change the time period of cooking according to the tenderness you desire. However, the meat becomes ready after reaching an internal temperature of about 160 degrees F.

4. Take out the rolls from the smoker and prepare for serving.

BEEF RECIPES USING ELECTRICAL SMOKER

SMOKED BRISKET WITH WORCESTERSHIRE SAUCE

SERVING SIZE: 1
SERVINGS PER RECIPE: 6-8
CALORIES: 200 PER SERVING
COOKING TIME: 20 HOURS 20 MINUTES

INGREDIENTS:

Beef Brisket- 13 lbs.

BBQ Rub (preferably Dizzy-Pig Red-Eye Express rub)

Vinegar- Apple Cider

BBQ Sauce- 1 1/2 cups (any brand)

Ketchup- 1 cup (any brand)

Steak Sauce- 3 tablespoons, A1

Worcestershire Sauce- 2 tablespoons

Brown Sugar- 1/4 cup

Black Pepper- 1 tablespoon (Fresh Cracked)

Paprika- 1 1/2 teaspoon ((hot smoked)

Chili Pepper- 1 teaspoon (Chipotle or Cayenne Pepper)

NUTRITION INFORMATION:

Carbohydrate – 3 g

Protein- 14 g

Fat – 14 g

Sodium - 680 mg

Cholesterol – 50 mg

DIRECTIONS:

1. Start by trimming off the excess fat from brisket and then clean it thoroughly.
2. After this, trim lightly the fat of fat cap side and with the help of a knife, separate the flat parts of the brisket.
3. Now, take a generous amount of BBQ Rub and sprinkle it in the areas, including both the flat parts and side points. After applying the BBQ rub, place a cut at fat-side down and place it on the Masterbuilt Smoker Grill with a thermometer probe inserted into it. The probe should be inserted in the thickest part of the brisket.
4. In the smoker, add three charcoal briquettes in the woodchip chute along with woodchips like hickory or Applewood.
5. Further, below the rack of brisket, place another pan filled with water and finally set the temperature of the Smoker to 250 degrees F.
6. During the smoking process, keep checking for woodchips in every hour. If you find less smoke, you can add more woodchips.
7. Now, as 2 hours of smoking are over, bring the temperature to 225 degrees F and again add 2 extra charcoal briquettes in the smoker.
8. Allow the brisket to slow cook for 10 additional hours and keep an eye on the internal temperature to reach 175 degrees F.

9. Once the internal temperature of brisket reaches to 175 degrees F, sprinkle Cider Vinegar over the brisket and again decrease the temperature to 200 degrees F.

10. Now, again cook the brisket for 8 more hours until the internal temperature reaches 200 degrees F.

11. Once the brisket reaches 200 degrees F, remove it from the smoker and place it over an aluminium foil.

12. Baste the brisket with sauce and let it again sit for 10 minutes in the smoker. After the heating of 10 minutes, remove it from the smoker and wrap it in a towel.

13. Now, place it in a cooler and let it rest for 2 more hours before you eat it.

SAUCE MAKING

1. To prepare a homemade sauce to baste the brisket, place a pan on the stove and keep the heat medium.

2. Add BBQ sauce, Steak Sauce, Worcestershire sauce and Ketchup in the pan and stir nicely.

3. In the pan, then add cider vinegar, black pepper (crushed) and brown sugar. Meanwhile, do not forget stirring the sauce.

4. Lastly, add smoked paprika, chili pepper and give the sauce a final mix.

5. Turn the stove heat to minimum and wait for the sauce to get thicken.

6. After 5 minutes, taste the sauce and add whatever you find less. Once done, remove it from the stove and the sauce is ready to baste the brisket.

SMOKED BEER BRISKET

SERVING SIZE: 1
SERVINGS PER RECIPE: 6-8
CALORIES: 296 PER SERVING
COOKING TIME: 15 HOURS

INGREDIENTS:

Brisket (split between point and flat)- 1 packet

Patriot's BBQ rub- 1 bottle

Brown mustard- 6 ounces

Apple juice- for bath and basting

Beer

NUTRITION INFORMATION:

Carbohydrate – 7 g

Protein- 35 g

Fat – 11 g

Sodium - 80 mg

Cholesterol – 101 mg

DIRECTIONS:

1. Take the brisket and trim its excess fat; Separate its point from the flat.
2. Now, trim the fat from a ¼ inch from the separated piece and then slather the brisket with spicy mustard.
3. Following the slathering, take a generous amount of rub and nicely massage the meat with it. After the rub massage, wrap it in a thin film and allow it to rest for 10 hours.
4. A few hours before, the 10 hours of resting is to over, prepare the Masterbuilt Smoker for smoking and add woodchips in the chute. You can use woodchips of choice, however, I prefer oak and hickory mix.
5. Further, the temperature of the smoker should be 230 degrees F and a pan full of beer, water, and apple juice is also needed to be kept a rack below the brisket.
6. Now, as the smoking process starts, keep a sharp on the smoke and keep adding woodchips after small intervals.
7. Keep continuing the process of adding chips until the thermometer reads 140 degrees as the meat's internal temperature.
8. Once two hours are complete spritz the meat using Apple Juice and let it smoke for another 2 hours.
9. Now, check the internal temperature and let it reach 165 degrees F. After the smoker has reached the desired temperature, perform the spritz one more time.
10. When the internal temperature reaches 195 degrees F, take out the meat from the Smoker and wrap it in a towel.
11. Let the meat sit for 30 minutes.
12. After 30 minutes, dig in and cut delicious and juicy slices out of the brisket to enjoy.
13. An average brisket takes 15 hours to cook, however, there is no set time. Therefore, always cook brisket according to the internal temperature.

SMOKED BEEF WITH ONION AND POTATO

SERVING SIZE: 1
SERVINGS PER RECIPE: 5
CALORIES: 266.6 PER SERVING
COOKING TIME: 5 HOURS 15 MINUTES

INGREDIENTS:

Beef brisket- 1 corned, (4 pounds)

Coca-Cola- 1 (7 ½ ounces can)

Garlic- 6 cloves, divided

Pickling spices- 4 tablespoons, divided

Bay leaves- 5

Golden potatoes- 1 1/2 pounds, tiny

Large onion- 1, coarsely chopped

Olive oil (extra virgin)- 2 tablespoons

Sea salt- 2 teaspoons

NUTRITION INFORMATION:

Carbohydrate – 18.2 g

Protein- 14.4 g

Fat – 14.9 g

Sodium - 778 mg

Cholesterol – 66.6 mg

DIRECTIONS:

1. Take the brisket packed in the bag and discard its liquid. Take a disposable aluminium pan and place the brisket into it. The pan should be 12-inch in dimension and it should be deep enough to hold the brisket.

2. Now, in the pan, empty the Cola Can and the packet of spice came with the brisket. If you did not get any spice packet with the brisket, then just increase the pickling spices up to 6 tablespoons.

3. In the same pan, add about 2 garlic cloves, and about 1 tablespoon of pickling spices. Cover the pan with aluminium foil and let it refrigerate for at least 3 hours. After 1.5 hours, turn the brisket upside down.

4. Meanwhile, the brisket is resting and grabbing all the required flavors, you need to prepare the smoker for smoking process.

5. Preheat it to 250 degrees F and add woodchips of your choice. While the smoker is being heated, add water to the water pan with some bay leaves, remaining garlic cloves, and remaining pickling spices.

6. Now, wash potatoes and onion. With skin on, place the potato in an aluminium foil along with the onion. Drizzle both potato and onion with olive oil and season them with salt and pepper.

7. Cover the whole from all the sides and place it on the first most grill rack of the smoker. Smoke it until the last hour of brisket smoking.

8. Now, in the smoker, place the pan of brisket. Make sure you keep it on the middle rack.

9. Let the brisket smoke for at least 5 hours.

10. After 2 hours, reduce the temperature to 225 degrees F and smoke for another 3 hours. When the internal temperature reaches 160 degrees F, take out the meat from the smoker and discard the aluminium foil.

11. Now, place the brisket again in the smoker without foil. Cook for good 30 minutes. After 30 minutes, remove both brisket and potato-onion parcel.

12. Let both, vegetables and brisket rest for 10 minutes for you to be able to handle.

13. Cut nice slices of brisket and serve it with Onions and Potatoes.

SMOKED LAMB IN MASTERBUILT SMOKER

SERVING SIZE: 1
SERVINGS PER RECIPE: 6-8
CALORIES: 320 PER SERVING
COOKING TIME: 14 HOURS

INGREDIENTS:

Lamb leg- 1, 6lb.

Garlic bulb- 1

Salt- 2 tsp

Grounded pepper- 2 tsp

Lemon juice- 2 Tbsp.

Olive oil- 2 Tbsp.

Bay leaf- 1, (crushed)

Lemon zest- 2 tsp

Paprika- 2 Tbsp.

Rosemary- 1 tsp

NUTRITION INFORMATION:

Carbohydrate – 1.4 g

Protein- 70.4 g

Fat – 69 g

Sodium - 604 mg

Cholesterol – 253.6 mg

DIRECTIONS:

1. I used Masterbuilt 2077515 smoker for this recipe. It is a spacious smoker and ideal for lamb leg.
2. So, let us start the recipe by adding ingredients to a mixer grinder or food processor to make a paste.
3. Give the ingredients a few rotations and see the consistency of the paste. Add, oil for consistency and thickness.
4. So, the paste is ready and now we will need to work out with the lamb leg. You will need to cut off and trim the excess fats.
5. Once you do so, the lamb leg is ready to be coated with the prepared paste. Now, coat the lamb leg with the paste and nicely wrap it with plastic film. Refrigerate the lamb leg for 45 minutes to start the smoking.
6. Meanwhile, the lamb leg is resting in the refrigerator, you prepare the Masterbuilt Smoker and add wood chips. I consider hickory as the ideal woodchip for lamb.
7. Now, as the smoker is heated up to 225 degrees F, place the lamb leg into the smoker. Place it on the top rack. The smoke timing should be 30 minutes per pound.
8. Also, insert a thermometer probe in the thickest part of the meat; it will tell the internal temperature which ultimately tells about the doneness of the meat.
9. When the meat thermometer is showing 150 degrees F as the internal temperature, it tells that the lamb is medium-prepared.
10. You can further smoke it to an internal temperature up to 185 degrees F. Once the thermometer reads 185 degrees F, remove the lamb from the smoker and let cook for 30 minutes.
11. Serve it with a lemon slice!

BEEF JERKY IN MASTERBUILT SMOKER

SERVING SIZE: 1
SERVINGS PER RECIPE: 3
CALORIES: 286 PER SERVING
COOKING TIME: 5 HOURS

INGREDIENTS:

Sirloin roasts (tip)- 2, 1 pound each (make sure all are equal strips of 1/4-inch)

Vinegar- 1 cup, apple cider

Kosher salt- 2 Tbsp.

Brown sugar- 2 Tbsp.

Molasses- 2 Tbsp.

Hot sauce- 1 Tbsp.

Onion powder- 1 tsp

Coca-Cola can- 2 (7.5 oz.)

Minced garlic- 2 Tbsp.

Jane's Krazy Mixed-Up Salt

Wood chips- soaked them in water

NUTRITION INFORMATION:

Carbohydrate – 13.9 g

Protein- 32.7 g

Fat – 10.5 g

Sodium - 2179 mg

Cholesterol – 81 mg

DIRECTIONS:

1. Before slicing the roasts into an equal piece of ¼ inches, freeze them for 30 minutes.
2. Now, take a saucepan and add vinegar, brown sugar, kosher salt, molasses, onion powder and hot sauce. Heat the mixture over medium heat until reduced.
3. Cool the mixture at room temperature and pour in one can of Coca-Cola and mix well.
4. In this prepared marinade of Coca-Cola and other ingredients, add the strips. Refrigerate the whole for 4 hours. If strips do not fully cover with marinade, you can turn them upside down in between the refrigeration.
5. After 4 hours of refrigeration, take out the meat from the marinade and rinse with water. Pat all the strips dry with the help of paper towels.
6. Leave these strips aside and prepare smoker. Heat the Masterbuilt Smoker to 180 degrees F and put the water pan filled with rest Cola Can. Into it, add water, minced garlic, and salt.
7. When the woodchips are fed, and the smoker is ready, place the meat directly on the smoker grill.
8. Smoke them for 3.5 hours and keep adding woodchips if necessary.
9. Check for rubber-like texture. If the meat has achieved the texture, they are ready as jerky.
10. Let the cool and store in a refrigerator.
11. You can use Jerky for 3 months.

ABOUT THE AUTHOR

James Houck is a health and fitness enthusiast who loves teaching people about healthy ways to lose weight and live the best life they can.

Over the years, he has studied what works and what doesn't in health and fitness. He is passionate about helping others achieve great success in their diet and exercise endeavor through his books and seminars.

His biggest satisfaction is when he finds out that he was able to help someone attain the results they've been looking for. In his free time, he loves to spend time with his 2-year-old daughter.

71269337R00038

Made in the USA
San Bernardino, CA
14 March 2018